SOUVENIR

A FANTASIA ON THE LIFE OF
FLORENCE FOSTER JENKINS

BY STEPHEN TEMPERLEY

★

★

DRAMATISTS
PLAY SERVICE
INC.

SOUVENIR
Copyright © 2006, Stephen Temperley

All Rights Reserved

SPECIAL NOTE ON MUSIC

The piano/conductor score containing the music for this Play is required for production and is available through the Play Service for $20.00, plus shipping. The nonprofessional fee for the use of this music will be quoted upon application.

For my mother, May Temperley

ACKNOWLEDGMENTS

I would like to express my gratitude to some of those who were instrumental in bringing *Souvenir* to the stage. First my agent, Bret Adams, without whose involvement there would have been no production. James Morgan and the York Theatre; Kate Maguire and the Berkshire Theatre Festival; Ted Snowdon and Janice Montana. I would particularly like to thank Tom Helm for his invaluable help with the musical aspects of the play. But more than any other, I would like to thank the play's director, Vivian Matalon, without whose constant encouragement over the years the play would not have been written. His production, as lyrical as it was hilarious, was all I could have hoped for and much, much more.

SOUVENIR received its Off-Broadway premiere by York Theatre Company (James Morgan, Producing Artistic Director), in association with Ted Snowdon, opening on December 1, 2004. It was directed by Vivian Matalon; the set design was by R. Michael Miller; the costume design was by Tracy Christensen; the wig design was by David H. Lawrence; the lighting design was by Ann G. Wrightson; the sound design was by David Budries; the assistant sound design was by Daniel Baker; the production stage manager was Jack Gianino; the assistant stage manager was Alex Finch; and the production supervisor was Scott F. DelaCruz. The cast was as follows:

FLORENCE FOSTER JENKINS .... Judy Kaye
COSME McMOON .... Jack Lee

SOUVENIR opened on Broadway at the Lyceum Theatre on November 10, 2005. It was produced by Ted Snowdon in association with Janice Montana and by arrangement with the York Theatre Company. The set design was by R. Michael Miller; the costume design was by Tracy Christensen; the lighting design was by Ann G. Wrightson; the sound design was by David Budries; the assistant set designer was Robert Monaco; the assistant costume designer was Colleen Kesterson; the assistant lighting designer was Aaron Spivey; the assistant sound designer was Phillip Peglow; the wig design was by David H. Lawrence; the general manager was Roy Gabay; the company manager was Bruce Klinger; the production stage manager was Jack Gianino; the production manager was Showman Fabricators; the stage manager was Alex Finch; and the musical supervisor was Tom Helm. The cast was as follows:

FLORENCE FOSTER JENKINS .... Judy Kaye
COSME McMOON .... Donald Corren

CHARACTERS

McM — Cosme McMoon. The former accompanist to Florence Foster Jenkins. At the time of the play he is a dapper man in his late 50s. He has been the resident pianist at an elegant supper club in Greenwich Village for some years. His audience comes to be entertained as much by his abrasive asides as his music.

FFJ — Florence Foster Jenkins. A wealthy society woman who, though she believes herself to be a great soprano, has no voice and is incapable of singing two notes in tune. Her belief in her talent, however, and her dedication to music and the art of singing is absolute. She behaves at all times as if she is a major vocal artist. There must be no hint of mockery.

TIME
1964 at first, returning to 1932 through the '40s.

PLACE
Framed by a paneled proscenium arch, the set is an elegant room which will become the various locations: the supper club; FFJ's music room in her suite at the Ritz-Carlton; the stage of Carnegie Hall; and a dressing room at Carnegie Hall. There are arches stage left and right. A piano stage right. A tall window in the upstage wall. For the music room, an elegant armchair and occasional table float through the left arch. For Carnegie Hall, the panels in the proscenium light. Other panels in the walls turn to reveal busts of Brahms and Mozart. For the dressing room, the armchair is replaced by a chaise. In the supper club, a stylized view of Manhattan is seen through the window.

8

SOUVENIR

ACT ONE

Darkness. A bold chord sounds on a piano. Then another and "One for My Baby" is being played. Light suddenly reveals McM in the supper club. Through a window behind him the towers of Manhattan are dimly visible. He sings:

McM.
> *It's quarter to three,*
> *There's no one in the place*
> *Except you and me.*
> *So set 'em up Joe,*
> *I got a little story*
> *You ought to know.*
> *We're drinkin' my friend*
> *To the end of a brief episode ...*

(Aside, sharply.) No, I don't take requests. *(Slyly.)* Not till I know you better.

> *Make it one for my baby,*
> *And one more for the ...*

Like anyone comes in a bar to hear grief from the pianist. You've no doubt got enough of your own. Still. Today's a kind of ... anniversary. So I'm not making any promises.

> *Well that's how it goes.*
> *And, Joe, I know you're gettin'*
> *Anxious to close.*
> *So thanks for the cheer,*
> *I hope you didn't mind*
> *My bendin' your ear.*
> *But this torch that I found ...*

OK, enough. I'm just down — not suicidal. I'll be right as rain by

9

tomorrow. *(Sardonic.)* My usual cheery self. *(With an abrupt change of tone, pulling himself together.)* OK. What else? A tune for her? Why not. Something she liked. What? Mrs. Foster Jenkins didn't care for cheap music and I doubt you want to hear Mozart. *(Gently, he starts to play "Crazy Rhythm.")* She liked this. Though she pretended she didn't.

Crazy rhythm, here's the doorway,
I'll go my way, you'll go your way,
Crazy rhythm, from now on we're through.

I counted up and realized it's twenty years today since she's been gone. Sometimes her name comes up. People still laugh. It's wonderful how everyone's so witty. They never heard her sing but they know enough to laugh.

Here is where we have a showdown,
I'm too high-hat, you're too lowdown,
Crazy rhythm, here's goodbye to you.

Tickets were like gold. *(Nostalgic.)* Those days! All the famous, smart people ... Cole Porter; Noël Coward; Elsa Maxwell; Walter Winchell; the Aga Khan ... They all came to hear her.

They say that when a highbrow meets a lowbrow
Walkin' along Broadway.
Soon the highbrow he has no brow,
Ain't it a shame, and you're to blame ...

(Lyrically.) When you sing ... you're like a prizefighter — though you don't use your fists. Just air. A thin thread of breath and that's it. You're mouthing words. Making noise. Your ears are ringing. Who knows what's coming out. You can never hear what others hear. A singer takes a good deal on trust. No two voices are the same. An *artist* ... finds his or her own true voice. Second-raters ... sound like everyone else. The real ones — you hear them — there's no mistaking.

They say that when a highbrow meets a lowbrow ...

People used to say to me: Why does she do it? I always thought the better question was: Why did I?

Everyone's got their arrival story. How it was when they first hit New York. Imagine. I'm twenty-four. *(Mock aggressive.)* Do that for me. It's 1927. New kid in town. Ready to tear up the sidewalks.

What's the use of Prohibition?
You produce the same condition.
Crazy rhythm, I've gone crazy, too!

(He rises to stand in the curve of the piano.) None of us had any

10

money. My friends and I. But no one felt poor. We were young. On the brink. About to do great things. Meantime we did this and that to get by. Back then when singers retired, they taught voice. Madame this, Maestro that. The old Hotel Ansonia crowd. I played for their lessons. At night I rehearsed my solo recitals — though I never gave any. And I wrote songs, tried to get them sung. Art songs. *(He shrugs.)* We did that then. So after five years of living this life, let me tell you, I was pretty damn tired. Her nephew Gil was someone I knew from … around. He said his aunt had a — "unique kind of sound." He said she needed someone to play. *(An elegant armchair and a small occasional table appear opposite the piano. MCM crosses to sit in the chair.)* She had a suite at the Ritz-Carlton. Sixteenth floor. I went there next day. She gave me a glass of sweet sherry and showed me into the music room. *(Enter FFJ. She halts beside the piano.)*

FFJ. Mr. McMoon …

MCM. … she said …

FFJ. … what matters most is the music you hear in your head. Don't you agree? The impossible ideal, as it were. The beauty not *quite* within our grasp. I have always had a great love of music. It's the music that draws me. It's the music that must come before all else. *(Sits on the bench.)* Let me be frank. While singing for friends, I have allowed myself to be accompanied by those who could not always give the music its due. Without wishing to give offense, for this my first *public* recital, I must be *(Gently.)* ruthless. I seek no reward from my singing — certainly no financial reward — no personal *réclame*. I assure you, this is no mere act of vanity.

MCM. Mrs. Foster Jen …

FFJ. *(Rises, crosses towards him. Politely.)* Please … let me finish. I know how it might seem: A woman like myself comes to a man like you — from out of nowhere — declaring herself ready to scale the pinnacles of the soprano repertoire. You could think me no more than a mere *dilettante* …

MCM. Mrs. Foster Jen …

FFJ. *(More politely.)* … no, please let me finish! I've sung many times for charity. In various drawing-rooms. Friends have been kind enough to compliment me on the depth of my feeling. Which is why it has now been *proposed* that my name on a handbill might prove an attraction. Among my own circle, you understand. I don't speak of the public at large. But still, enough to fill a modest hall. Which is rather exciting, don't you think? What I seek — have sought, am seeking — is a colleague, a collaborator, a soul mate.

McM. Mrs. Fost …

FFJ. *(Even more politely.)* No, please, you *must* let me finish! Let me say at once that I would not expect you to undertake such a task without a remuneration that I intend to be fully commensurate with your dignity. Now. What do you say?

McM. *(Cautious.)* It's by no means impossible … what you ask.

FFJ. *(Grateful.)* I thank you for that. You have given me hope.

McM. It's a matter of polishing, you say — ?

FFJ. And perfecting. Refining. May I confide in you, Mr. McMoon? You won't think me foolish? Some weeks ago I dreamed I was singing in public.

McM. Yes?

FFJ. Do you know what it was that I sang? In my dream? The famous aria of the Queen of the Night. *(Reverent.) Der Hölle Rache kocht in meinem Herzen! Tod und Verzweiflung flammen um mich her!* The very words produce chills. *(She shudders. Utters a small shriek. McM is at a loss for words.)* You are familiar with that particular aria?

McM. *Zauberflöte.*

FFJ. *Comment?*

McM. *Magic Flute.*

FFJ. Exactly! And who do you think was in the audience, smiling up at me, encouraging me? Mr. Mozart.

McM. Mr.…?

FFJ. Mozart! I would hardly call myself a follower of Mr. Freud but the meaning seemed all too apparent. Did I have it in my voice, I wondered? Few sopranos are equipped to tackle the Queen of the Night. As you're no doubt aware, the aria's range is extensive. I had my doubts. One is only human after all. *(Laughs. Stops herself abruptly.)* However — and this is almost too uncanny — the next day — the very next day, Mr. McMoon! — while riding in a taxicab on Lexington, I found myself in a slight collision. The f above c burst from me spontaneously.

McM. *(Bewildered.)* The f above c?

FFJ. Passersby were enraptured, amazed. I stepped from the wreckage a new woman. But enough talk. Let's take the plunge. Shall we make music? Shall we see how we suit? *(Inviting him to sit at the piano.) S'il vous plaît? (She crosses to a cabinet from which she brings a sheaf of music, returning with it to the piano. Turning over sheet music for individual arias:) La Fanciula?* Perhaps not before lunch. *Così?* So grateful to the voice. *Lucia?* She presents a fascinating problem, does she not? How to sing in Italian while at the same time suggesting a Scottish burr. Please. Should I mention some special favorite — shout it out! *(Scanning the contents of an album.)* *Bohème*, *Faust*, *Rosenkavalier*. Each delicious in its way. Ah! Dear *Rigoletto*! "Caro Nome"? Perfect. You are acquainted, I assume, with the work of Mr. Verdi? Modern music isn't to everyone's taste, I know. *(She settles "Caro Nome" on the piano then hurries back to the curve, readying herself to sing.)* Mr. McMoon? *À vôtre plaisir.* *(She nods gravely to him. He plays a brief introduction. On cue, to his astonishment, she unleashes a series of wild shrieks and hoots.)*

> Gaultier Malde!
>
> No me di lui sia ma to.

(At the first note he snatches his fingers from the keys. As she continues to sing he rises from the bench to run around the piano to get a closer look. As if to make sure, he snatches off his glasses.)

> Ti scolpisci nel core inamorato!

(She freezes.)

McM. *(Aside: in utter disbelief.)* What … was … she … hearing? What? What was going on in her head? Was I … Was I in the presence of mere delusion or a kind of … dementia? *(He takes another look at her, replaces his glasses and hurries back to the bench. He begins the introduction to the main body of the aria. She awaits her cue, clearing her throat demurely, settling her jacket, enjoying his feel for the music.)*

FFJ.

> Caro nome che il mio cor,
> Festi primo palpitar,
> Le delizie della mor
> Mi dei sempre rammentar!
> Colpensier il mio desir,
> A te sempre volera.
> A ha! A ha! A ha! A ha!
> A ha! A ha! A ha! A ha!
> A ha! A ha! A …

(After the first couple of notes, her singing again veers off into shrieks and hoots. When at last it becomes impossible he stops.)

McM. *(Shouts.)* Sorry! Sorry. I'm ah got … Sorry. Let's. OK!

FFJ. *(Explodes.)*

> A ha! A ha! A ha! A ha!
> A ha! A ha! A ha! A ha …

McM. *(Even louder.)* Wait!

FFJ. Yes?

McM. Let's see. *(He falls silent.)*

FFJ. *(Puzzled but polite.)* Yes, Mr. McMoon?

McM. OK, I have to say I'm hearing a certain want of … accuracy.

FFJ. Accuracy?

McM. Some intonations are perhaps not *quite* what is written.

FFJ. *(Bewildered.)* Not…?

McM. You don't hear it?

FFJ. I only hear the music. *(He picks out the vocal line with some emphasis.)*

McM. Listen. Yah da da da da da *dah!*

FFJ. *(She crosses away, singing her own version.)* Yah da da da da da dah! *(Turns back to him, pleased with her success.)*

McM. *(Correcting her.)* Yah da da da da da *dah!*

FFJ. Yah da da da da da dah!

McM. *(Repeats.)* Yah da da da da da *dah! (He rattles the final key with his little finger, sounding the note emphatically.)* Dah!

FFJ. Dah! Dah! Dah!

McM. *Dah!*

FFJ. *(Rapturous.)* You see, this is what I want! This is what I hoped for! You have quite an attractive voice, by the way. I wonder if you ever considered developing it. Or do you find yourself content merely playing piano? I could never be. But then, I have a temperament. *(She crosses to stand over him, pushing him out of her way to tap out the note he has been sounding. She sings the wrong note. Repeats this twice more with different wrong notes. Satisfied that all is as it should be, she hurries back to the curve of the piano.)* Where were we, *cher* … *(Bestowing on him the title.)* Maestro? *(Reverently, she cues him to begin. He repeats the note to cue the cadenzas.)*

A ah! A ha! A ha! A ha!

A ah! A ha! A ha! A ha!

A ah! A ha! A …

(He struggles grimly to keep her in time, particularly as she starts to get carried away. He stops playing abruptly, covers his face with one hand. She stands blinking, like one who has come from bright sunshine into a darkened room.) You must forgive me if I get carried away and obfuscate the tempi. But this is exactly what I hope you'll stop me doing. I put myself entirely in your hands. *(She waits expectantly.)*

McM. Well, sure, OK …

FFJ. I want you to be harsh, Mr. McMoon.

McM. Harsh? Well … how can I say?

FFJ. You must be brutally honest.

McM. *(Takes a deep breath.)* It seems to me ... Some notes are not perhaps *quite* ... secure?

FFJ. Secure?

McM. Not *quite.*

FFJ. *(A realization dawns.)* Ah! *(She settles herself in the chair.)* Have you perfect pitch, Mr. McMoon?

McM. Pitch?

FFJ. Pitch.

McM. *(Confused.)* I have relative ...

FFJ. *(Consoling.)* Ah. Never fear. It's no disgrace. Though it must be inconvenient.

McM. You are ... have ... ahm ...

FFJ. Perfect pitch. Yes.

McM. Uh-huh.

FFJ. You find that hard to believe?

McM. *(Hastily.)* No no, no, no.

FFJ. I wouldn't blame you if you did. There are not many of us who are so blessed.

McM. *(Rises from the bench abruptly, anxious to change the subject.)* You spoke of a recital, Mrs. Foster Jenkins. That you're preparing for a recital. I'm wondering exactly what it is you mean by that.

FFJ. *(Confused.)* Well ... a recital. *(Explains as if to a child.)* You would play. I would sing. Songs.

McM. And the scale of it?

FFJ. *(Laughs.)* Oh, I see! A modest affair. A few select friends. Some two hundred or so. Certainly not more than three or four. Here at the Ritz. In the ballroom. To benefit some of my favorite charities.

McM. So this is not something the general public ...

FFJ. If some music lover should wish to attend, I would *hope* they could be seated.

McM. Still you don't expect, say, to be *reviewed?*

FFJ. *(Pityingly.)* You mean those dreadful newspaper people? Would they be welcome? On no account. No. If you hunger to see your name in print, Mr. McMoon, you'll be disappointed, I'm afraid. If it's *ambition* ...

McM. *(Aside.)* And *that's* where I had a choice. Right then. I could have made some excuse, walked out into the afternoon and gone about my business. But she was so ... absolutely, transparently ... sure of herself. Not in a vain way — she was right about that. She believed the way a child might believe. It was touching somehow. And it seemed to me it would be intolerable if I didn't try to protect her. So was that her vanity or mine? *(Sitting to play.)* Let's go on, shall we?

FFJ. Bravo! *(She rises excitedly, crossing to the end of the piano, eager to hear what he has to say.)*

McM. *(With more confidence.)* Each note has its own ... value, Mrs. Foster Jenkins. When we see *b flat* on the page, for example, we must be certain *that's* the note we sing. *(He sounds b flat.)* It's an absolute. Not something about which we can be ... evasive.

FFJ. *(After a moment's thought.)* I think it's possible to be *too* analytical, don't you? Nothing is more detrimental to good singing than this modern mania for accuracy. That was never true in the past. Music came from the heart. You say the notes are absolute, but what are they, after all? *(She crosses away from the piano.)* Signposts left by the composer to guide us. A vocal artist must claim some latitude.

McM. Mrs. Foster Jenkins ...

FFJ. *(Turns to him.)* Yes?

McM. *(He rises to cross to her.)* I think it's best to enter into any new relationship with a clear head, don't you? I wouldn't want to make a commitment now only to disappoint you later.

FFJ. You have other engagements that would take up your time? Or plans perhaps to travel?

McM. *(Amused by her assumption.)* I'm afraid my bank account won't permit me much in the way of trips right now.

FFJ. I'm glad you're speaking frankly, Mr. McMoon. Let me do the same. *(She returns to the chair, regally:)* I was not always as you see me. Before my father's death, I found myself compelled to make my own way in the world. When confronted with the necessity to choose between art and personal comfort, I left my childhood home and supported myself — laboring many long hours over the keyboard — to teach what I could of the great mystery and joy that is music to the children of Wilkes-Barre, Pennsylvania. Believe me, I'm very conscious of the extreme privilege my income provides. *(With a hint of temptation.)* One of the sweetest uses of my present relative affluence is making what I have available to others. *(A pause as he weighs her offer.)*

McM. This recital — *(Emphatically.)* which is *not* to be reviewed ... Gil mentioned a date some, what?

FFJ. Six weeks from today. Exactly.

McM. *(Aside.)* One recital. Just one. What harm could it do? Maybe it wasn't exactly what I'd hoped for ... But. Was it my fault I had the whole of that month's rent to pay since my latest room-

16

mate moved out somewhat abruptly after a dispute over the meaning of monogamy? I was already twenty-nine. You can't be "promising" indefinitely. *(Turns to her.)* I'm not quite sure why you think I can do so much for you, Mrs. Foster Jenkins. You've hardly heard me play. Perhaps my style wouldn't be suitable … to show you to your best advantage. Your particular voice, you see … Your voice, Mrs. Foster Jenkins … *(Unable to continue, he falls silent.)*

FFJ. Mine is not a large voice, Mr. McMoon. What I have is something much more rare: *(She rises regally, achieving her full height before speaking.)* — the true coloratura. I don't flatter myself. My own particular gift is purity of tone. Though this might be hard for you to believe, when I was a young woman my singing was actively discouraged. *(She crosses away from him, agitated.)* I have known doubt. The dark night of the soul. Music saved me. Dear me! My hands are trembling. You must not think me precipitate, Mr. McMoon, but somehow I feel my whole life has been a preparation for this meeting. There is a vibration between us, artistically speaking. I cannot help but feel that our partnership is somehow fated.

McM. *(Aside, as he makes his way back to sit at the piano.)* I thought of my friends. What they'd have to say. Of walking out on the platform with her. Sitting at the piano. Lifting my hands to play. I thought of the rent. *(To her.)* Shall we try picking up…? *(He starts to play the introduction.)*

FFJ. *(Suddenly.)* Stop! Stop! You must stop!

McM. Pardon me?

FFJ. This is wrong! Wrong! *(She advances on him, one hand extended for the music.)* If you please.

McM. *(Disappointed, he gives her the copy of "Caro Nome.")* I'm sorry, I …

FFJ. A time like this calls for sacred music. *(She searches for a particular piece. Settles new music on the piano.)* Here. This is the music I would sing with you. Years ago it was the piece that awoke my soul. The *Ave Maria.* Mr. Gounod's, of course. I leave Mr. Schubert's to the mezzos! *(Amused by her joke, she takes her place at the end of the piano.)* I should mention that this has always been my final encore. I find my audience has come to expect it. *(A warning that he should be strong.)* Often it provokes tears. Beginning please at bar twenty-two. The *"Sancta."* *(He plays.)* Let us start with what is best, Mr. McMoon. For only good can follow.

Sancta Maria! Sancta Maria!
Maria!

Ora pro nobis,
Nobis peccatoribus,
Nunc et in hora,
In hora mortis nostrae,
Amen! Amen!

(She sings with considerable feeling, rapidly losing herself, the time, and any semblance of pitch. He does all he can to keep playing. She ends triumphantly. Blackout. Lights come up on Cosme in the club. His expression speaks volumes.)

McM. *That* was how we began our association. We were together twelve years. So we met — what? More than thirty years ago. Jesus! Ancient history. I'm a relic. She's a myth. The crazy lady who couldn't sing. We spent many hours rehearsing. Many, many hours. When the great day came, she sang a total of twenty-four songs and ... *(Despairingly.)* five encores! Despite all the false starts and dropped notes, one selection followed another till at last we were done and she was taking her bows. *(He rises as the chair and table return. He crosses to sit in the chair.)* I snuck back up to the music room. My job was done. I figured I'd change and slip out. *(Enter FFJ, in a state of great excitement.)*

FFJ. Dear heart ... there you are! Come and meet my friends! Please, please, please! They were simply *overawed* by your playing. *(Gratefully.)* Finally. To find an accompanist on one's own level! It has been ... a gift! Now we must *really* get to work.

McM. What?!

FFJ. There's so much to be done!

McM. *(He rises, startled.)* You're not going to do this again?

FFJ. *(In a state of great excitement.)* It seems a large part of the audience simply begged for our return. People had tears in their eyes. I'm not surprised. I myself saw some literally stop their mouths with handkerchiefs. To stifle their sobs, I assume. Naturally I will insist that nothing nothing nothing! be done without you. We must get to work *tout de suite.* Tomorrow!

McM. You mean ... do this *again?*

FFJ. Yes of course.

McM. Rehearsing and so on?

FFJ. *Mais oui.*

McM. *(He crosses away from her.)* I'm very sorry ... I really don't think I can. I mean ... I don't.

FFJ. You don't?

McM. Unfortunately there are other claims on my time. Other ...

18

demands. Other commitments. Other. *(A longish pause. Eyes narrowed, she studies him closely. Sits on the bench.)*

FFJ. I think I see what's going on.

McM. You do?

FFJ. How could I not?

McM. *(Panicked. Assuming the worst.)* See … I'm sorry, but you know … I did my best! *(He has crossed in a conciliatory manner towards her. Now she rises, advancing on him, forcing him back.)*

FFJ. You naughty, naughty boy.

McM. Pardon me?

FFJ. I won't allow this.

McM. You won't?

FFJ. In the six weeks I've known you, I've come to care about you, dear heart. About your future. As a friend.

McM. It's my future I'm … I mean everyone's saying I should concentrate more on my … own … *(Crosses despairingly to the piano bench.)* What am I saying?

FFJ. This is worse than I thought. For years I allowed the opinion of others to stand in the way of *my* musical progression. My greatest fear was that I should look somehow ridiculous. Can you imagine? Those who should have been my support sensed my fear and used it to … silence my voice. It was only after much internal struggle I was able to break free. Now here you are caught in that selfsame trap. Others might stand idly by, but I'm not one to watch you throw away such an opportunity. Cosme — if I may call you that.

McM. I'm grateful, of course …

FFJ. If you turn your back now you will simply break my heart. I won't be unreasonable. No, no, no. We'll rehearse when you want. At most a few hours a day. Here. In the music room. I think it's pleasant enough. And you will write your music. *(Sees that he is tempted.)* Surely you won't refuse an association that could be of such benefit to us both? Surely you won't do that?

McM. *(After a pause.)* I guess we could … give it a shot.

FFJ. Bravo! *(Impassioned.)* Bravissimo! You'll see how well we shall do together. *(She starts to exit.)* An ongoing, working …

McM. Partnership. *(She returns to make her meaning absolutely clear.)*

FFJ. In the musical sense. Not, of course, in the public sense. *(Exits talking.)* Now, you must come next door as soon as you're changed. Everyone's dying to meet you! *(He sits at the piano. The stage returns to the club.)*

McM. It was like magic. Word just spread. Every time she sang more people wanted to hear. You couldn't keep them away. *(He rises to stand in the curve of the piano.)* As word got around, the audience changed. It wasn't just her Park Avenue friends anymore. It was more like the crowd you see at the fights. We were at the Ritz-Carlton so there was a certain level of restraint. Even so I'd see them crying. When she sang. Doubled over in their seats. Hitting each other, convulsed. There were gasps, sudden shrieks. They'd jump to their feet and run up the aisles. You'd hear doors banging. And the sound from the lobby of people laughing. When they got themselves under control, they'd make their way back to their seats, flushed, still wiping tears away. You see a lot from a piano bench. Meanwhile, Madame Flo was lost in the music. So far as she was concerned, the people running for the doors were just too moved to stay. Too overcome by emotion. *(Returning to the bench.)* At the end there were bravos and flowers. And afterwards she'd serve sherry and her friends would talk about what she wore. So one way or another everyone had a pretty good time. *(He pauses, troubled.)* Though I worried. In case a day might come when the balance tipped, when her friends were outnumbered by that other, crueler part of the audience. When the ones coming to laugh set the tone. *(Pulling himself together.)* We were rehearsing. She loved to rehearse. She rehearsed more than anyone I ever knew. We were preparing for that year's recital. She was late. Which wasn't like her. Wasn't like her at all … *(He swings into a jaunty version of "Crazy Rhythm." The armchair and table return. Enter FFJ wearing furs and carrying her hat, bag and gloves.)*

FFJ. What on earth are you playing?

McM. I was just noodling.

FFJ. No but really, what is that? *(He stops playing.)*

McM. Nothing — a song.

FFJ. A song? What kind of song?

McM. Nothing you'd like.

FFJ. *(Pretends to be shocked.)* You mean a popular song? *(She crosses to deposit her bag and gloves on the occasional table beside the chair.)*

McM. Kind of thing people dance to. A song.

FFJ. It has words, this song?

McM. Pardon me?

FFJ. Words. *(He rises to go to the music cabinet.)*

McM. Shall we get on? *(She throws off her fur stole, letting it drape over the arms of the chair.)*

FFJ. All in good time. *(Giggles.)*

20

McM. *(Suspicious, crossing towards her.)* What? What is it?

FFJ. What is what?

McM. You've got a look about you.

FFJ. I can't think what you mean.

McM. Like the cat that got the cream.

FFJ. Cream indeed.

McM. Has something happened?

FFJ. What would they be, these words?

McM. You're not telling me?

FFJ. *(Simpers.)* For example. *(Annoyed by her teasing manner and quietly gleeful air he recites matter-of-factly.)*

McM. OK. Well … *"Crazy rhythm, here's the doorway."*

FFJ. Oh, please do play! Won't you? You were playing so nicely before I came in.

McM. It's really nothing much …

FFJ. Please!

McM. OK. *(Crosses to sit at the piano. Accompanying himself he sings.)*
     Crazy rhythm, here's the doorway.

FFJ. *(Repeats the phrase high in her voice, in an almost waltz-like rhythm.)*
     Crazy rhythm, here's the doorway.
(Eager to learn more.) Yes?

McM. No. It's syncopated … See? *(Establishing the time.)* One-two. One-two *(Emphasizing the rhythm as he sings.) uh! …*
     Crazy rhythm, here's *the* door*way.*
     Uh! I'll go my *way* you'll *go* your *way.*

FFJ. *(Repeating without rhythm.)*
     uh! I'll go my way you'll go your way. Uh!

McM. No! No, you don't sing … that's just … That's where the beat is. You don't sing that. See? *(He pounds out the rhythm on the notes, continuing:)*
     Uh! They say that —
     Uh! when a highbrow meets a lowbrow
     Walk*in' a*long *Broad*way …

FFJ. *(Rises to correct him emphatically.)*
     Walk*ing* along Broadway …

McM. Walk*in'* … *Walkin' along Broadway* …

FFJ. *(Trying out the stresses.) Walkin'? Walkin'? Oh, walkin'! along Broadway* … Oh, I see! Yes. *(Crosses towards the piano.)* Quite a cheeky little tune, *n'est çe pas?*

McM. The accents are falling on the off-beat. There's a spring to it.

FFJ. *(Reality dawning on her.)* Is this what they call "jazz"? Is it? Goodness, Cosme! *(Caresses the piano.)* You've quite shocked the Bechstein.

McM. Music is music.

FFJ. And people sing this song and they dance? Is that what happens? Your friends, for example. When you and Kurt — such a personable young man! — when you and he are entertaining young ladies. You bad boys.

McM. *(Embarrassed.)* Shouldn't we get to work?

FFJ. *(Crossing away from him, oblivious.)* I could almost picture myself singing it. I imagine it would create quite a sensation.

McM. Here at the Ritz? … I don't know. Your audience expects something different.

FFJ. Ah! But what if we were to find ourselves with a different kind of audience?

McM. Different?

FFJ. Different.

McM. In what way?

FFJ. Suppose we suddenly found ourselves with more seats to sell?

McM. More … seats?

FFJ. Many more.

McM. But you've … Madame J, you've been sold out for weeks.

FFJ. True.

McM. Why would you need more seats?

FFJ. So that many more music lovers could pay their two-forty to attend.

McM. You've already got five hundred coming. Isn't that enough?

FFJ. Think of my charities, Cosme! Think what such a box office boost could mean.

McM. Boost?

FFJ. Boost. You see, it's been proposed … Quite out of the blue. That we move our recital. To a larger … venue. Which is rather exciting. Don't you think?

McM. But … *(He rises and crosses to her.)* I thought you were happy here at the Ritz.

FFJ. Up to a point.

McM. I thought you liked the intimacy of the ballroom.

FFJ. Yes and no.

McM. Exactly what are we talking? How much larger?

FFJ. Believe me, we will make quite a splash. There is considerable anticipation among those in the know.

McM. And you just…?! I mean, it's arranged?! Just like that?!

FFJ. It's come as a shock. I quite understand.

McM. I should say so.

FFJ. I was telephoned, Cosme. And this was *proposed.*

McM. Proposed? *(Crosses away, returning to the piano bench.)* What was proposed? Move us where? The Hippodrome?

FFJ. Not. Quite.

McM. Where? *(Terrified, he jumps to his feet and rushes back to her.)* Dear God — tell me where!

FFJ. *(Reverently.)* Town Hall.

McM. *(Appalled.)* Town Hall?

FFJ. It's been proposed we move our recital there, Cosme. Where they have guaranteed there will not be a single empty seat. Not one!

McM. But…!

FFJ. Of course I knew I had a following. I'm not blind after all. But I must say, I had no idea I was quite so … popular! *(She sits in the chair.)*

McM. I can't believe what you're telling me.

FFJ. I could hardly believe it myself.

McM. *(His hysteria growing.)* I mean, what have I been doing all this time? All this rehearsing! This isn't easy for me. I'm trying to do … what's right for you. *(He snaps, lashing out at her.)* I could just let you *sing!* You know? But I don't. Because I worry. And because I do the decent thing everyone assumes I'll just go along…! with whatever … crazy…! *(Becoming speechless.)*

FFJ. *(To calm him.)* Shh! Cosme, dear Cosme, think what's at stake! In these perilous times. With so many in need. How can I refuse? We must all try to do some good in the world.

McM. *(His vehemence born of desperation.)* But at what *price?*

FFJ. *(Startled.)* I beg your pardon?

McM. At what *price?*

FFJ. I don't understand.

McM. Your artistic standards. What of them?

FFJ. *(She moves to him, alarmed.)* Come dice? *(Now that he has her attention he pursues his advantage, improvising frantically.)*

McM. Your voice in a barn like Town Hall?

FFJ. Barn?

McM. They didn't tell you? About the acoustics? I mean it's famous. For how you can't hear.

FFJ. You can't?

23

McM. You think you've gone deaf.

FFJ. Deaf?

McM. *(Advances on her, backing her into the chair.)* To go from our little room to that great huge monster…! It's something that should be approached gradually. Very, very gradually. If at all.

FFJ. Surely, we can rehearse. Prepare.

McM. And if *strain* should be induced? What then?

FFJ. *(Unnerved.)* Strain? *(With one hand she caresses her throat.)*

McM. It could undermine all we've worked for. I can't allow that. Won't. I don't care what they say.

FFJ. *(Her other hand goes to her throat.)* Strain?

McM. Strain. *(Seeing that he has won, he crosses back to the piano.)* Mrs. Foster Jenkins, listen, if your concern is extra revenue — wouldn't the same result be achieved by adding another recital here at the Ritz? At least that way there won't be any …

FFJ. Strain. *(Silence. Humbly:)* What can I say? You have saved me from myself.

McM. *(Modestly.)* Well.

FFJ. *Mille grazie, signor buon fortuna.*

McM. *(Sits.) Prego.* I guess.

FFJ. To abuse my voice is unthinkable. After all, one is not a trombone.

McM. Exactly!

FFJ. We shall add two more recitals to our present schedule.

McM. Two…!

FFJ. *(To indulge him.)* Very well — three. But no more! How right you are, Cosme. And how very wise. There is no good reason to move. There is every reason to stay. I shall explain to Town Hall. Let them find someone else to sing in their barn! Some mezzo or other. *(Gathering her possessions from the table.)* Forgive me for not consulting you first. It shall not happen again. Strain! *(Exit FFJ. He watches her go. Lights return to the supper club. The chair and table disappear.)*

McM. How could she *not* know? She had to hear the laughter. Didn't she? If people assumed I was in on the joke — that I knew that they knew — maybe they figured she knew, too. You know what it's like in this town. There was a lot of speculation over martinis. It was all too sophisticated for words. Hell, I didn't care! Let them think what they like. I kept telling myself it was only part of my life. A means to an end. The money I made working with her kept me going all year. I had a patron. I never saw her in spring or summer. Never saw her outside of the music. I had all this free time.

24

Time to do something remarkable. Astonishing. Time to become whoever it was I was supposed to be. So I wrote songs. All kinds of songs. Happy songs. Sad songs. Short songs. Long songs. *(Ruefully.)* Songs no one wanted to sing. *(He pulls himself together.)* We had our niche at the Ritz Carlton. Not exactly ideal, but it was OK. If I couldn't stop her making a fool of herself, I could at least limit the damage. From day one she begged me to let her sing the Queen of the Night. It was her one big ambition. Her one big dream. Don't ask me why. I said not yet. You're not ready. I'm not ready. Nobody's ready. *(He plays some of the vocal line of "Der Hölle Rache," emphasizing its vertical leaps and impossible intervals, landing heavily on the high notes.)* How could she think she could sing it? How was it possible? She had no voice. No ear. No musicianship. Nothing. Beyond a certain feeling. True, that had never stopped her before. Or me either. But the Queen of the Night was like crossing a line. Going from having an oddly endearing blind spot, an eccentric lack of perspective to … what? Madness? *(Enter FFJ as if in a trance. After lingering for a moment in the entrance arch, she crosses slowly to the piano. As she does, McM rises, bracing himself for bad news.)*

FFJ. I've been invited to make a record. *(He sits abruptly.)* Me! It seems they think I could do much to popularize good music.

McM. I don't understand, Madame J. Who's invited you to make a record?

FFJ. The record company.

McM. Yes, but which one?

FFJ. There's more than one? Oh, well, I should think this must be the record company that appeals to lovers of good music. They want me to choose which particular aria will show my voice to its best advantage. At last I shall have a chance to really *hear* myself.

McM. *(Appalled.)* Oh my God!

FFJ. The time has finally come to perfect dear Mr. Mozart's beloved aria for the Queen of the Night.

McM. *(Rises, crossing to her.)* I wonder if that's really the best choice. For a record.

FFJ. It is the *perfect* choice! Think, Cosme, think! In days to come, when my voice is not perhaps quite so strong as it is now, to be able to hear it as it once was! In all its glory! A lovely souvenir.

McM. But think, Madame J … a record … can be so misleading.

FFJ. You're not going to be stubborn, are you? It would mean so much to me. Please! Please!

McM. What if you were to be … disappointed?

FFJ. Disappointed? In what way?

McM. The sound in your head, what you hear when you sing, could that ever be caught on record?

FFJ. Cosme, I'm not a fool. You talk to me as if I'm a fool. *(She sits.)* Dear heart, of course I know that! How could I not? Of course I know it will be but a shadow. But why not at least record what can be recorded? I will imagine the rest. Think of all I could learn! The ... what do you call it? The microphone will be quite, quite objective.

McM. *(Passionately.)* It will *not* be objective. It will diminish. *I* am objective. *I* am your ears.

FFJ. Dear Cosme! So that's it. You think I would rely on you less? How could that be? When this device will merely allow me to enjoy something of what everyone else hears. Is that such a bad thing?

McM. Suppose ... Just suppose what you hear is not what you expect? Suppose there are aspects of your vocal production that are not ... *(Unable to complete the sentence, he turns to walk slowly around the piano till he stands near the keyboard. He turns to face her.)* Sometimes, what we hear inside ... with our inner ear ... that is the truth.

FFJ. You have touched me, Cosme. Truly touched me. I had no idea you had such feelings of ... protection towards me. *(She rises, crosses towards him.)* But you must see that you can protect too much. It is from our greatest challenges that we learn most. Without the risk of failure there can be no success. You say the microphone will diminish. So will doubt. Art cannot be ruled by caution. The Queen of the Night awaits. My breath is her life! *(She is on her way out but turns to admonish him one last time.)* We have come this far together. Let's not falter now. *(Exit FFJ. Anguished, McM sits on the bench. The stage darkens rapidly. A bright light picks him out.)*

McM. *(With a growing sense of disbelief.)* A record?! Hear herself! The Queen of the Night? *(As the light goes out on him it snaps onto the victrola on the opposite side of the stage. The record plays; the Queen of the Night's aria is in progress. A light now picks him out as he listens to a phrase. Another light finds FFJ as she hears the next. Light spreads to the rest of the stage as the aria continues. McM is in despair; FFJ is ecstatic. Overwhelmed by the beauty of the recording, FFJ mimes those patches she thinks are particularly successful, turning to him with an air of triumph, joining her recorded voice to sing the final note full out. It is over. The record rasps on the turntable.)*

FFJ. *(Exhaling.)* Well! *(She rises to lift the needle, dragging it across the surface of the record.)* Perhaps it is not *all* I could have hoped for, but on the whole I must say I'm quite pleased. *Quite* pleased. *(Crosses towards him.)* It has spirit. *Con brio, molto vivace!* Yes. My one reservation is that there is a place — you know, where it's … *(She demonstrates, singing a series of notes.)* — and I'm not sure but I think *something* goes awry. I'm surprised you didn't notice yourself, you naughty boy. Because really, if there is an imperfection — no matter how small — we must be allowed to correct it before it's sent for sale. Record that side over. *(She is struck by his silence.)* Cosme, do you intend to say nothing?

McM. I'm just thinking. It's a lot to take in.

FFJ. *(Crosses away from him to sit in the chair.)* My friends will want copies. Yours will, too.

McM. *(Covers his face.)* Oh my God!

FFJ. I'm told it will be available at Altman's — among other places — so it's quite important that everything be perfect. You know how critical people can be. To say nothing of the newspapers. I've kept them away from our recitals but I can do nothing to stop them availing themselves of a record. I've seen how unpleasant they can be when they have the opportunity to criticize a person above their social sphere. Goodness knows I'm no snob. *(Gently.)* Look how well you and I get on! But you can't expect some gutter journalist to have an appreciation for — or knowledge of — the music of Mr. Mozart. Let me try to find … *(She rises to cross to the victrola, lowering the arm onto the record. She makes two attempts to locate the suspected flaw — scratching the record in the process — without success. On the third try, however, she finds it.)* There! There! *(She lifts the needle.)* You heard it? There *is* something not quite right. I'm sure of it now. No doubt in a recital such a teeny-tiny flaw would not be remarked on. The presence of the artist would bring the hearers along. *(She crosses away from him.)* But that microphone is so unforgiving, so unaware of nuance. I see that now. Not that I didn't believe you when you warned me but still. It's all rather humbling. But there can be no doubt: *(Sternly.)* The piano is not *quite* with the voice. *(Outraged, he spins on the bench doing his best to control himself. She sees his reaction and crosses towards him to comfort him.)* No doubt you were unnerved to find yourself away from our dear music room. Your concentration was not all it should have been. You must *not* blame yourself. Not for one moment. *(He whirls back, pounding the keyboard to make her stop. Startled, she jumps back.)*

McM. *(With the exaggerated calm that comes from rage.)* It's not right? There's a mistake? You want it to be right?

FFJ. Naturally. I mean … don't you?

McM. Don't I? Oh, *don't* I?

FFJ. Cosme, what *is* the matter?

McM. Let's get it right, then. Shall we? We'll just get it *right.* OK? *(He plays a series of notes, the first of the rushing arpeggios that characterize the aria. Harsh.)* Do it! *(She attempts to sing the notes. He bangs the bass notes to interrupt her.)* No! *(He repeats the musical phrase.)* Do it! *(She attempts it again. Again he bangs the keys.)* No! *(He repeats the phrase.)* Do it! *(She attempts it again. Again he bangs the keys.)* No! *(He repeats the phrase.)* Do it! *(She attempts it again. Again he bangs the keys.)* No! *(He repeats the phrase but this time she interrupts.)*

FFJ. Cosme, you must not punish yourself further!

McM. No No No! Can't you hear? Don't you hear? Why don't you *listen? (Playing.)* Yah dah dah dah dah dah *dah!* Why can't you hear? For God's sake! What is wrong with you? Yah dah dah dah dah dah DAH! *(On his feet.)* Goddamn it, just sing what's *written,* you SILLY … WOMAN! *(A long pause. She has been badly shocked. She turns her back on him, crossing slowly to sit in the chair. He realizes that he's gone too far. He sits. When he does speak he does so gently.)* You said I should be brutal. Right at the first. *(She glares at him.)*

FFJ. I did not ask you to be rude!

McM. *(Rising to appeal to her.)* I want you to sing as well as … you can. I would hope you believe me when I say that. Because I mean it. Sincerely.

FFJ. I am *not* a silly woman!

McM. Perhaps I spoke too abruptly.

FFJ. You have *some* sense of shame.

McM. Yes.

FFJ. There is nothing wrong with *my* ear. Nothing at all.

McM. No.

FFJ. Nothing. I want that clearly understood.

McM. Yes.

FFJ. I am known for my ear.

McM. Yes.

FFJ. Nothing, nothing, nothing. *(There is a silence between them. Unsure how to continue but anxious to comfort her he steps towards her. Pointedly, she turns away, He turns, crossing slowly towards the piano. Behind his back, her head turns to follow him. Sensing her look, he turns once more. She turns away. He slumps onto the bench where he sits despondent. After a moment, his fingers find the keys. Very gently, he starts to play the verse to "Crazy Rhythm," singing very quietly:)*

McM.

> *Every Greek, each Turk and each Latin,*
> *The Russians and Prussians as well,*
> *When they seek the lure of Manhattan*
> *Are sure to come under your spell.*

(He looks over at her. She is puzzled by his actions and hesitates a moment.)

FFJ. Nothing. *(She turns away again. He perseveres.)*

McM.

> *Their native folk songs they soon throw away,*
> *Those Harlem smoke songs they soon learn to play.*
> *Can't you fall for Carnegie Hall?*

(He rises to his feet to appeal to her. Spoken:) Madam! *(She ignores him. He sits and carries on.)*

> *Call it a day and we'll say …*

(He plays the chorus out of time in a laconic, free-form manner.)

> *Crazy rhythm, here's the doorway.*
> *I'll go my way, you'll go your way.*
> *Crazy rhythm, from now on we're through.*

(He turns to look at her. She turns away, still too hurt to meet his eye.)

> *Here is where we have a showdown.*
> *You're too high-hat …*

(Spoken, directly to her.) I'm too low down. *(She looks at him, softens slightly. She stands, crosses slowly to the piano. After a moment he continues.)*

> *Crazy rhythm, here's goodbye to you.*
> *They say that —*
> *When a (Indicating her.) highbrow …*
> *Meets a (Indicating himself.) lowbrow*
> *Walkin' along Broadway.*
> *Soon the highbrow she has no brow,*
> *Ain't it a shame?*

(Lifts his hands from the keys and speaks.) And I'm to blame …

FFJ. *(Gently.)* You bad boy! *(Relieved, he starts to sing with a cautious optimism.)*

McM.

> *What's the use of Prohibition?*
> *You produce the same condition.*
> *Crazy rhythm, I've gone crazy too.*

(The songs stops.)

FFJ. Ridiculous song.

McM. *(Swinging into the chorus joyously.)*
> *Crazy rhythm, got me goin',*
> *Crazy rhythm, there's no knowin'.*
> *Crazy rhythm, why I'm here with you ...*

FFJ. *(Interrupts him.)* Those are not the words, Cosme! For goodness' sake, you might at least sing the right words. *(Quotes the lyric.)* They say that when a *(Indicates herself.)* highbrow meets a *(Indicates him.)* lowbrow, walkin', walkin', WALKIN'! along Broadway. Aren't you going to play? Do it! *(He picks up the tune, racing to keep up when she joins in.)*

McM.
> *Soon the highbrow he has no brow,*

BOTH.
> *Ain't it a shame? And you're to blame.*

FFJ.
> *What's the use of Prohibition?*

McM.
> *You produce the same condition.*

BOTH.
> *Crazy rhythm, I've gone crazy, too!*
> *(They fall silent; glad to be reconciled.)*

FFJ. *(Gently.)* Now that song may be called silly!

McM. We'll do it for your next record.

FFJ. There are so ... *(She crosses around the piano to take his hand. Pressing it to her bosom.)* You must know, dear heart, how very grateful I am for all that you do. So very grateful. So very, very grateful! *(Impulsively, she kisses his hand, then presses it to her heart.)*

McM. *(Aside.)* My friends all bought the record. *(Blackout.)*

ACT TWO

In the darkness, a chord sounds on the piano, which intro-
duces "I Guess I'll Hang My Tears Out to Dry." Light finds
McM at the keyboard. He sings:

McM.
> *Dry little teardrops,*
> *My little teardrops,*
> *Hanging on a string of dreams.*
> *Fly little mem'ries.*
> *My little mem'ries.*
> *Remind her of our crazy …*

The record did very well. Surprisingly well. Amazingly well. So we
made more. The damn things played all over the East Side. My
name on labels going round and round. She became an honest-to-
God celebrity. She was much imitated at parties. You can imagine.
All the time I'd been playing for Madame Flo my friends used to
kid me but it was OK. Pretty much. But after the recordings the
kidding got pretty intense. It was non-stop. Like there was nothing
else they could talk about. Someone would ask: *(Snooty voice.)* How
are rehearsals going? *(Snooty laugh.)* Or they'd suggest *stuff* she
could sing. And they'd all laugh. They couldn't stop laughing. So I
figured what the hell.

> *Friends ask me out,*
> *I tell them I'm busy…!*

I made new friends. Less musically inclined. *(He rises, circling*
around the piano from above till he finds his place in its curve.) I kept
telling myself that Madame Flo was only part of my life. I still had
my own work. I wrote more songs. Began an opera. Tore it up.
Traveled some. Bought groceries. Fell in love. Then one day my
suits didn't fit. You can only live on hope so long. Somewhere along
the line you start wondering — is this it? Is this all I rate? Am I
crazy to keep writing songs no one wants to sing? Maybe they're
right. Maybe they really *are* trash. Maybe I'm no better than her.
And I would suffer. Because there's a thing that happens when the

31

rest of the world doesn't see your life's work the same way you do. When you realize you've become kind of a joke. You can try to fight the contempt. Deal with the rolled eyes. The sniggers. Or you can adjust. Lower your expectations. Either way you're not going to be happy. *(He returns to the bench.)* Then I'd look at Madame Flo. She never needed to adjust and she was never unhappy. With her, it was the opposite. She got happier. She never had any doubts. She went right on singing. With me there beside her. And I found myself ... admiring her. I found myself hoping some of her certainty would rub off on me. *(He launches into "It all Depends on You.")*

> *I can be happy,*
> *I can be sad.*
> *I can be good or*
> *I can be bad.*
> *It all depends on you ...*

As time went by, I moved beyond admiration and began to wonder if she wasn't some kind of genius. Her folly was so stupendous you had to admire its scale. Like the Chrysler Building. I found myself wondering if she hadn't discovered some new kind of form. If her performances weren't really commenting on our assumptions of what music is. And isn't. *(Defiant.)* I got so I almost preferred the way she sang. I heard Rosa Ponselle ... and something was missing.

> *I can save money,*
> *Or spend it,*
> *Go right on living,*
> *Or end it.*
> *You're to blame, honey,*
> *For what I do.*

(Belligerent.) Who's to say that if one note follows another we call it a tune but a different note makes us wince? Who made up the rules? *(More reasonably.)* I never said any of this to her — she wouldn't have seen how it applied. So I said it to myself. I'd have long theoretical discussions with the bathroom mirror on the meaning of counterpoint. I hardly knew there was a war on.

> *I know that*
> *I can be beggar,*
> *I can be king.*
> *I can be almost any old thing,*
> *It all depends on you!*

In the autumn of our twelfth year together we were about to give the first of our annual recitals at the Ritz. September, 1944. We were rehearsing … *(He plays the introductory chords to "The Musical Snuffbox." The chair and table appear. Enter FFJ. She holds sheet music and is nodding out of time. When she sings she seems distracted, her sense of pitch even more erratic than usual.)*

FFJ.

> Ah ha ha ha ha ha ha ha ha ha ha ha,
> Ah ha ha ha ha ha ha ha ha ha,
> Ha hah!

McM. *(Sounds a note.)* You should be here, Madame J.

FFJ. Isn't that what I sang?

McM. It's *c*. *(He sounds it again. She tries it out.)*

FFJ. There! The piano must be out of tune. It seems to be happening more and more. As if it's made too much music in its day. It can't find the notes quite so easily now. Though its heart is willing.

McM. I'll give you your cue. *(He repeats the introduction to cue her. She doesn't sing. Instead, she puts the music in the cabinet and sits in the chair.)*

FFJ. Cosme, I want you to promise that if you ever, *ever!* should come to detect any hint in *my* voice that it is not as it was, you will tell me at once.

McM. But, Madame J …

FFJ. Never mind if I deny it. Never mind if I accuse you of ingratitude or disloyalty.

McM. Madame J …

FFJ. No matter how painful such a truth might be, I would want *you* to be the one to tell me. Don't let me be like the Bechstein.

McM. You sound pretty much the way you always have.

FFJ. You're not just saying that?

McM. What is it? Has something happened?

FFJ. You don't hear it, dear heart, but there are times I find myself having to chase after notes that used to come quite effortlessly. Though I have done my best to protect my voice, time still takes its toll. Since I must face the day my music will desert me, I wonder … *(She rises and crosses to the piano, not speaking till she is still.)* … would it have been better not to have been so blessed?

McM. You're not thinking of retiring?

FFJ. *(Surprised and amused at such a thought.)* Retiring? Why would I think of retiring?

McM. You were saying your voice …

FFJ. Rhetorically. I still dream of reaching a wider public. *(She moves away, pensive.)* Though would it be prudent at this stage of my career to leave myself open to...? Jealousy is a terrible thing. I'm not so blind but I can see how others might portray me. *(She faces him across the piano.)* All those smart people. Who haunt first nights at the opera in order to jeer. You know the type. I've been so very fortunate. So very protected. You have given me so much. *(She turns from him, moving away, steeling herself.)* Dear Cosme, something rather exciting. Almost ...

McM. Almost? Almost what?

FFJ. I hope you're not going to be cross.

McM. *(Rises and crosses towards her. Suspiciously.)* Cross? Why should I be cross?

FFJ. Well exactly! You'll no doubt be as thrilled as I am. You see, it's been *proposed* ...

McM. *(Clutches his side to assuage the sudden sharp pain.)* Yes?

FFJ. A grand recital. To honor our fighting men. I'm told there are many lovers of good music in the Armed Forces. Did you know? I must say I had no idea.

McM. *(Interrupting.)* Proposed?

FFJ. Well, yes.

McM. *(Insistently.)* A special concert here at the Ritz?

FFJ. Not ... quite. When it was proposed ... *(Evasive.)* what was proposed ... I couldn't help but feel what a feather in my cap it would be. To say nothing of yours. To be able to say, yes, I have played ... *(Afraid to say the words aloud, she completes her sentence with a knowing jerk of her head, backwards, over her shoulder.)*

McM. Played?

FFJ. Played. *(Repeats the gesture.)*

McM. *(A sudden terror grips him.)* Oh dear God.

FFJ. Somewhere very ... Somewhere almost ... How shall I say...?

McM. What? What place?

FFJ. *(Dancing with glee.)* Cosme, it has been proposed that I give a recital at Carnegie Hall! *(He flattens himself against the piano in horror.)* That's what's proposed! I couldn't be more surprised.

McM. You keep saying proposed! *Who* has proposed?

FFJ. *(Patiently, spelling it out.)* The people who want me to give the recital. Really, Cosme, who else would propose it? *(She sits in the chair.)* My only concern has been that you should think it a *good* thing. I get quite overcome. I can't help it. *(A sudden thought lifts her to her feet, one hand to her throat. When she has risen, she continues.)* I wonder if this is what it means to be nervous? I feel an unaccustomed tightness in my throat. *(She vocalizes.)* It does seem strange, with all my experience, that I should be assailed by nerves like any beginner, but there we are. Now you know. I must sit down. *(She does. In a daze, he makes his way back to the bench and sits.)* I must say, Cosme, this isn't quite how I'd hoped you'd react. It's rather a red-letter day. I do wish you'd say something.

McM. Carnegie Hall? I heard Heifitz there! I heard Galli-Curci there.

FFJ. *(Rises.)* Soon you'll hear me. Us. And the best thing of all — the icing on the cake as it were — *(Advancing on him.)* I'm determined to sing something of *yours! (Appalled, he jumps to his feet and retreats.)*

McM. No! Please…!

FFJ. You're not to thank me. *(Almost an accusation.)* It's what you *deserve.* Heavens! You've written so many *lovely* songs over the years. Lovely, *lovely* songs. It's a scandal they're not heard. I could almost think you don't want them sung the way you hide them away. Remember how I had to beg and beg before you'd let me have them printed. Unless I had even I wouldn't know them. *Tiens!* The world has waited long enough. What better time to introduce your "Serenata Mexicana"?

McM. *(Clutching at straws.)* "Serenata"'s really for a mezzo …

FFJ. But these days I'm finding warmer colors, don't you think?

McM. Is it really showy enough?

FFJ. Not one more word. I insist.

McM. You don't have to do this.

FFJ. But I want to.

McM. You know how long it takes you to get a song. When is this proposed concert proposed to be? How long do we have to prepare?

FFJ. I have it by heart already.

McM. *(Sinks hopelessly to the bench.)* I can't do this. I really can't. *(She glares at him.)*

FFJ. *(Harsh, forcing him to look at her.)* Cosme! *(Startled, he turns. She points at her eyes, as if to hypnotize him.)* Look at me! I have absolute faith in you. I know you will rise to the occasion. It's been a shock. But once you get used to the idea, you won't feel so overwhelmed.

McM. *(Pleading.)* Does it have to be Carnegie Hall?

FFJ. I think I could die happy knowing I'd sung there. I truly do. And you will hear your lovely "Serenata" as it should be sung. *(She sings a capella, as if lullabying a favorite child, adding a little dance of*

her own invention:)
  Remember, niño,
  The love that we knew that summer.
  When you murmured "forever!"
  Beside the shining sea.
(She ends with a flourish, waiting expectantly.)
McM. *(Appalled.)* I don't know what to say.
FFJ. You mustn't be afraid, Cosme. Always remember. *(She crosses to stand beside him, her hand on his shoulder.)* I shall be there at your side. I'm beginning to believe — so long as we're together — there is nothing we can't do. *(Exit FFJ. Lights change to the supper club.)*
McM. *(Lyrically.)* Carnegie Hall! *(Down to earth.)* We sold out almost as soon as the concert was announced. Two-dollar-forty seats were scalped at twenty bucks. We worked very hard to get everything right. She had a whole new wardrobe designed. A different costume for every song. We spent hours in the music room. It all had to be perfect. Every note. *(He plays a brief introduction to "Violets for Your Furs," which he goes on to sing with an elegant understatement and simplicity.)*
  It was winter in Manhattan,
  Falling snowflakes filled the air.
  The streets were covered with a film of ice.
  But a little simple magic
  That I'd heard about somewhere
  Changed the weather all around
  Just within a trice —

  I bought you violets for your furs
  And it was spring for a while, remember?
  I bought you violets for your furs
  And there was April in that December.

  The snow drifted down on the flowers
  And melted where it lay.
  The snow looked like dew on the blossoms
  As on a summer day.

  I bought you violets for your furs
  And there was blue in the wintry sky.
  You pinned my violets to your furs
  And gave a lift to the crowds passing by.

36

You smiled at me so sweetly
Since then one thought occurs —
(With a lyrical intensity.) When I got to the hall there were flowers everywhere. *(He rises, crosses to the curve of the piano.)* I walked over from my place on East Fifty-Third. The sidewalks were crowded with service men. Some with girls, or in groups, on the prowl. I even saw some at the box office among the mob waiting for returns. Two thousand people were turned away. I ran into some … ex-friends talking to one of those boys in uniform fresh from someplace you never heard of. He couldn't stop yapping about how disappointed he was he couldn't get in. He'd heard from everyone this was the big thing in town. He was shipping out in a couple of days and who knew where he'd end up. I had a spare ticket. I gave it to the boy with the smile and wondered what life had got planned to temper his enthusiasm. He was so pleased he could hardly talk. So that was something.

      Inside, I could hear her warming up and again I wondered — how much did she know? And more to the point — what would she do once she caught sight of the crowd in the house? *(He returns to sit on the bench.)* Would her folly, or madness — whichever it was — be enough to keep her safe? And what of my part in it all? No matter what anyone said, I was playing Carnegie Hall. My music would be heard in Carnegie Hall. That was something to be proud of, wasn't it? Some profit from all those spent years.

You smiled at me so sweetly,
Since then one thought occurs,
That we fell in love completely,
The day that I bought you violets for your furs.

Singing is a kind of dreaming in public. But were we heading into a nightmare? In Mexico, that last summer with Kurt, he slipped getting into a boat and hit his head. He told me later it was like he was somewhere else, watching us pull him out of the water and try to revive him. He was quite calm in that place. Before he decided to breathe. And come back to all the mess and smells and joys of life. I never really understood what he meant till I walked out on that stage. Something so overwhelming you don't ever forget. It stays with you forever. Right here and now I could almost be back in that hall. *(He rises to demonstrate.)* I made my entrance. I remember thinking, who made the lights so bright? I reached the piano. I played a brief intro. *(Takes his place at the piano with a certain formality.)* There was a hush. Then … *(He gestures to where she will appear.)* she entered. *(There is a dramatic bump in the lights. Recessed lights in the proscenium snap on. Enter FFJ. She wears an elaborate gown, a long chiffon scarf trailing from one hand. The Carnegie Hall audience bursts into enthusiastic applause. She sinks into a curtsey. She crosses to the piano, smiling, preparing herself to sing. Turning to MCM, she inclines her head gravely. He plays a chord.)* First she sang — FFJ.

> *Elle à dans sa main la baguette*
> *Ou tinte la clochette,*
> *Ou tinte*
> *In clochette*
> *Des charmeurs?*

(She nods imperiously to mark the downbeat, then dances away from the piano. As he plays, she puts one hand up to her ear to demonstrate the listening to distant bells. She takes it down when she sings her reply. And so on through the brief excerpt from the aria, though she gets a little confused near the end.)

> *Ah ha ha ha ha ha ha ha ha ha, ha ha ha ha!*
> *Ah ha ha ha ha ha ha ha ha ha, ha ha ha HA!*

(She freezes after the high note.)

MCM. The "Bell Song"! *(There is an enthusiastic burst of applause from the Carnegie Hall audience. She curtseys deeply, hand to heart. She faces the crowd, thrilled, trembling, then bolts for the exit. As she goes, the stage returns to the club — as it will at the end of each aria.)* The crowd seemed ready to play its part. A lot of the regulars were there. I'd been concerned that at Carnegie Hall things might turn ugly. But it looked like they were going to keep the first-timers in line. I was quite hopeful. My "Serenata" was next. She'd told me she had something planned. Something special. She wouldn't say what. She wanted it to be a surprise. Of all the costumes she was going to wear that night, this was the only one I hadn't seen. I said a prayer. I began the introduction. *(He plays a flourish. Enter FFJ wearing an elaborate Spanish costume, brandishing a single maraca. She dances across to the piano. She poses to show off her costume. When he sees her, MCM fumbles at the keyboard, unnerved. She gathers herself to sing.)* FFJ.

> *Mi corazón, recuerda!*

(She brandishes the maraca, then tosses it in a high arc to her other hand.)

> *Bosos robados del verano.*

(She repeats the maraca shake and toss.)

Cada momento blando
Su promesa del amor.
(She turns on McM, stalking him with her maraca.)
Verano, como se regaza.
(Her final flourish comes near to hitting him. He pulls his hands from the keys and leans away. She tosses the maraca and continues.)
Cuando flores fueron.
(After a lyrical moment she advances to the front brandishing her maraca like a club.)
Les estrellas y usted lejano.
Todavia canto serenade.
(Huge applause which she acknowledges graciously, extends her arm to indicate McM, leading the applause for his piece. Shyly, he stands to take a bow. She mouths "He wrote this song!" to the audience. They bow to each other. He sits and strikes up her exit music. She dances her way off. The stage returns to the club.)
McM. There it was. Though you could hardly call the performance ideal, you can't say it didn't happen. Let me tell you I was pretty damn proud. My song had been sung in Carnegie Hall. My God! I was up there with Brahms. She sang one of his next. A song dear to her heart, since it so perfectly expressed her own view of singing. Though art must thrill the soul, its true purpose was to teach. The tension was mounting. Spontaneous eruptions traveled through the house. They were on the edge of their seats, hungry for her return. *(As he plays the opening chords of "Die Mainacht" the lights bump back on for Carnegie Hall. If anything, they are brighter than before. Enter FFJ with a certain solemnity, wearing a costume suggesting a scholar.)*
FFJ.
Raise thy voice to the heavens,
If thy dreams be strong.
But! Singer, if thou canst not dream...!
(She holds the note for an absurd length of time.)
Then leave thy song ... unsung!
A VOICE. *(From the house.)* You said it, lady! *(Laughter. She curtseys, mouths "Thank you" to her unseen admirer. There are some ironic cheers. She turns to McM, thrilled. The audience applauds enthusiastically. Exit FFJ, blowing kisses, peering into the darkness offstage.)*
McM. She didn't hear laughter. She heard cheers. Bravos. The lights kept getting brighter. So it seemed. Brighter and brighter. I didn't see how they could be so bright. Out in the house they were scanning their programs. Strangers turned to each other, eager to

compare their favorite moments. Veterans showed newcomers how to save their strength. How to rest between numbers. How to hide behind the seat in front to catch their breath. How to stop their mouths with handkerchiefs to stifle their laughter. How to cut and run when things got too much. All the old tricks. We came to —
(Enter FFJ with a shriek. She wears a gown of gold covered in jewels. She spies an imaginary casket downstage and hurries to open it.)
FFJ.

> *Ah! Voiçi justemente*
> *Au fond de la cassette,*
> *Un miroir. Oh!*

(She brings an imaginary mirror out of the casket and examines her face, overcome by her beauty.)

> *Comment n'être pas coquette?*
> *Comment n'être pas coquette?*

(She adorns herself with imaginary rings and a tiara as the piano gathers itself to launch her into the main body of the aria, "L'air des bijoux.")

> *Ah! je ris de me voir*
> *Si belle en çe miroir,*
> *Ah! je ris de me voir*
> *Si belle en çe miroir,*
> *Est-çe toi, Marguerite?*
> *Est-çe toi? Réponds-moi*
> *Réponds-moi,*
> *Réponds, réponds, réponds moi!*
> *Ah…!*

(After an endless wavering trill, she stops on a shriek.)
McM. "The Jewel Song"! *(The audience gives her an ovation. Some laughter is heard. She curtseys gratefully, moved by their enthusiasm. The audience cheers. She exits blowing kisses, stopping only to clasp her hands above her head in a gesture of victory.)* There was one last hurdle before intermission. I'd begged her to give it a miss. The audience was right on the edge. I'd already seen some bolt for the doors. The rest were hanging by a thread. But she insisted. If she was happy in her work, she wanted those who heard her to be happy too. If Mr. Sinatra had his bobby-soxers, why should she be denied the same kind of adulation? I thought it was playing with fire. But there it was. "Adèle's Laughing Song." *(Enter FFJ, dressed as a maid, holding a large, showy fan. She scampers across to the piano and strikes a coquettish pose. The audience reacts explosively. Meanwhile, McM plays the vamp for "Mein Herr, Marquis.")*

FFJ.

> *Oh, noble sir,*
> *How far you err*
> *You're really not discreet.*
> *What a funny — ah ha ha!*
> *You amuse me — ah ha ha!*

(She starts the laughs almost in time but gets slower and more labored with each repetition.)

> *If I laugh, sir — ah hah ha!*
> *Pray excuse me — ah ha ha ha!*

(There is an uproar in the house. She is encouraged, gesturing with her fan to have the audience join in.)

> *What a funny — ah ha ha!*
> *You amuse me — ah ha ha!*
> *Ah ha ha ha!*
> *Hah ha ha ha ha ha ha ha!*
> *Hah ah hah! Ahhh — ha!*

(She battles her way through the final cadenzas, ending triumphantly. Applause, cheers and laughter from the house. She bows and exits, blowing kisses to the house and waving.)

McM.   In the intermission she was skipping about like a girl. I tried to get her to rest. She still had some big stuff to get through. We began the second half with … *(He can hardly bring himself to name it.)* the Queen of the Night. They were screaming. Yelling *Brava! Diva!* The applause went on and on. Till their hands hurt. To cover the laughter. She took it in stride. She figured Mr. Mozart was having the same effect on them he had on her. Once the house quieted down, she went on to other old favorites. Then she threw in something unexpected. A tribute. To our fighting men. *(Enter FFJ wearing a G.I. cap and uniform. She comes to the front of the stage and salutes. The audience roars at her. She marches as she sings.)*

FFJ.

> *Down went the gunner, a bullet was his fate*
> *Down went the gunner, and then the gunner's mate*
> *Up jumped the sky pilot, gave the boys a look*
> *And manned the gun himself as he laid aside*
> *The Book, shouting:*
> *Praise the Lord, and pass the ammunition!*
> *Praise the Lord, and pass the ammunition!*
> *Praise the Lord, and pass the ammunition*
> *And we'll all stay free!*

(The audience is clapping in time.)
> *Praise the Lord, and swing into position,*
> *Can't afford to sit around a'wishin'*
> *Praise the Lord, we're all between perdition*
> *And the deep blue sea!*
> *Praise the Lord, we're on a mighty mission!*
> *All aboard! We're not a goin' fishin',*
> *Praise the Lord, and pass the ammunition*
> *And we'll all stay free!*

(Applause. Laughter. She salutes again, makes the "V for victory" sign and exits, waving.)

McM. The crowd was reckless. The long effort to control themselves had finally pushed them over the edge. Tallulah Bankhead had hysterics and had to be carried out of her box. In the orchestra they were waltzing in the aisles. Fights broke out in the mezzanine. In the balconies they waved their arms from side to side. Handkerchiefs fluttered down from the upper tiers. *(He stops. When he continues, it is with a sense of dread, with solemnity.)* The house was stifling. We were into the encores. They wouldn't let go. They kept yelling for more. They knew what was coming. So did I. *(McM begins the introduction. Enter FFJ, wearing wings and a small tinsel crown. The audience reacts deliriously to her appearance. She makes shushing gestures, grateful for their enthusiasm but entreating silence for the music. She sings:)*

FFJ.
> *Ave Maria,*
> *Gratia plena,*
> *Dominus tecum:*
> *Benedicta tu.*
> *In mulieribus,*
> *Et Benedictus*
> *Fructus ventris tui, Jesus.*
> *Sancta Maria …*

(As she sings the laughter grows till she can't help but hear it. She is startled. Almost accusingly, she turns to McM, who stares at the keys. She adjusts her wings, provoking a roar from the house. She shades her eyes to look out. A rhythmic clapping begins, joining the laughter, growing louder and louder. She is bewildered, panicked, squinting in the increasingly bright light. She hears the audible derision coming from the house and sings from her heart. Soon nothing can be heard but clapping and laughter. Then, abruptly, an eerie silence. She continues to mouth the words, facing the house. Blackout. In the darkness

we hear the piano, McM playing "One for My Baby" out of time. Lights come up. A chaise is in place opposite the piano. Enter FFJ. He senses her presence and stops.)

FFJ. Why didn't you tell me?

McM. *(Unable to answer directly.)* They gave me a piano. *(A pause.)* So I could warm up. *(She crosses in silence to the piano. Cosme observes her, uncertain how best to proceed in the face of such disaster.)*

FFJ. *(Simply.)* You didn't tell me. Why didn't you tell me?

McM. *(After a pause.)* Toscanini dresses here. *(A pause.)* Right in this room.

FFJ. When I begged you.

McM. Think of that.

FFJ. Cosme, why didn't you tell me?

McM. What? What is it, Madame Flo?

FFJ. Have I been so ... *(She can hardly bring herself to say the word.)* foolish?

McM. *(Not to be deflected from his course.)* I thought it went ... very well.

FFJ. Have I?

McM. Really. Very well.

FFJ. How could you let me make such a fool of myself?

McM. I don't ... you just had a huge success. Out there. Huge.

FFJ. *(Turns away from him.)* Don't!

McM. Didn't you hear them at the end?

FFJ. At the end. They ... *(She sits on the chaise.)* Cosme, I heard them...!

McM. They were just ... loving you. Didn't you hear? It was ... quite huge. Didn't you hear that?

FFJ. I thought ... *(She turns from him. He rises.)*

McM. What? What did you think?

FFJ. I didn't know what to think!

McM. Let me tell you ... I don't mind admitting I was quite nervous. Before we began. I didn't know how they were going to take you. But, boy! They really loved you.

FFJ. Did they?

McM. Loved. You. A whole big concert hall full of strangers and they loved you.

FFJ. Did they really?

McM. Really.

FFJ. Cosme, you would tell me?

McM. *(Crosses towards her.)* On my way in I was talking to a soldier

43

— just a kid — he was tickled pink he was going to get to hear you. He didn't know where he'd end up. But wherever he goes he's going to have some happy memories after tonight. He'll be one happy G.I.

FFJ. Happy?

McM. Oh, yes! Very happy! You could hear them. They were just eating it up. You could hear them. Didn't you hear them? Didn't you hear how happy they were?

FFJ. I heard, I thought ...

McM. What did you hear?

FFJ. I thought they were laughing, Cosme. Were they? Were they laughing? You expect that in "The Laughing Song." That's to be expected. But the "Ave"? My beloved "Ave"? Why would they laugh? I don't understand.

McM. *(Comes closer, choosing his words with care. Very gently.)* You've heard of nervous laughter? You know how when an audience sees something just overwhelming and they can't deal with their emotion ... the only way they can release it sometimes is to laugh. You must know that. That's so well-known. I'm surprised you don't know that. You could ask anyone and they'll tell you. How many singers today can provoke that kind of reaction? I'll tell you — very few. There are very, very few.

FFJ. I saw them with handkerchiefs ... I'd seen that before but I thought ... I imagined something quite ...

McM. Well, of course. You wouldn't want them just sobbing, would you? Just bawling their eyes out.

FFJ. I didn't know what was wrong. I thought I was in voice.

McM. You were. You were in *fine* voice.

FFJ. Some things I always sing well but one or two I thought I'd never sung better. The Mozart, for example ... *(He sits beside her.)*

McM. Unforgettable!

FFJ. Dear Cosme...! *(She brings her handkerchief up to cover her eyes and sobs as if her heart is breaking.)*

McM. *(Tenderly.)* I don't know why you're upset. I thought you'd be happy. Why aren't you happy? Look what you did. You had a triumph. *(Emphatically.)* You gave those people something they'll never forget.

FFJ. *(Speaking with difficulty, through her tears.)* You wouldn't ... ever tell me things ... that weren't true ... would you, Cosme? For whatever reason. You wouldn't ever ... lie to me?

McM. I would never do that. Never.

FFJ. You promise me? You swear?

McM. *(Holds up one hand.)* I swear on all that's holy I would never lie to you. Never. Do you believe me?

FFJ. I'm …

McM. Do you? *(Mock rough.)* You better believe me! *(He pretends to box with her as with a child. She laughs abruptly. They laugh together. She dries her tears.)*

FFJ. I was so afraid …

McM. I don't know what you think went on out there.

FFJ. I didn't know what to think.

McM. You're overtired. From all the excitement.

FFJ. I felt … I felt I was lost. I didn't like that.

McM. No one likes that.

FFJ. I felt … *(With a burst of energy, rising.)* I *do* feel quite tired!

McM. You're bound to be tired. Look what you did! *(She makes her way to the piano, touches it reverently.)*

FFJ. Toscanini really dresses here? If only he could have heard me tonight! I imagine he would have had much to say. *(Shyly.)* Cosme, if Mr. Mozart had been here, do you think he'd have been pleased?

McM. I think he'd have been very pleased. Very.

FFJ. I do hope he'd have been pleased. And Mr. Verdi. Mr. Gounod. All of them. *(She sits on the bench, allowing her fingertips to caress the keys. Almost mournful:)* Since I was a girl, you know, I've dreamed of such a night. And now it's gone. It was ahead of me. It was there to be hoped for. But now it's over. It's in the past. A memory. If only we could live in the music forever, Cosme. If only it could go on and on. But of course it can't. Of course it has to end. *(With an abrupt change of tone.)* I must get changed! *(She rises to face him as he sits on the chaise.)* You will come to the party, won't you? You won't desert me. *(Solemnly, he rises to face her.)*

McM. As if I could.

FFJ. *(Almost shyly.)* I should so like to leave with you. Perhaps you would escort me to our reception? Unless …

McM. *(With a formal tenderness.)* I should be honored. *(He offers his hands.)* Truly.

FFJ. *(Taking his hands.)* Thank you. Dear Cosme. Thank you. For telling me the truth. In my heart of hearts I never really doubted that you would. *(Exit FFJ. He watches her go. The stage transforms to the club.)*

McM. *(Abruptly.)* Within a month she was dead. *(Contemptuous of such sentimentality.)* No, it wasn't the concert! It had nothing to do with the concert. I've read how it broke her heart — how she

never sang again and the rest of the garbage. *(Crosses to the curve of the piano.)* But let's face it, she was no Violetta. No Butterfly. She was not the kind of character who dies of heartbreak. What I do know is she called me bright and early *next day! …* to make plans for next year's recitals at the Ritz. The day she died she met some friends for lunch at Schrafft's. *(Matter-of-factly.)* They were going to a matinée of … *Harvey.* But she'd already seen it. So she said good-bye and stopped by Schirmer's to order some music. Which was where her heart gave out. They told me she was conscious for a while. The manager sat her in a chair and brought her a glass of water. She said it was a nuisance as she still had rather a lot to do. She said she was feeling better and it was probably the creamed chicken. Then … she was gone. They closed the store till the ambulance arrived. We were supposed to rehearse later that day. Toscanini sent flowers. *(With some surprise.)* I missed her. I really missed her. *(He returns to his place at the piano where, very gently, he plays a few notes from "Crazy Rhythm.")* I was surprised how much I missed her. *(With a new determination.)* She always said her singing didn't count unless she was under the spell of the music. You know? Only the music mattered. And the thing about music is … about singing … finally … like she said that first day, what's important is what you hear in your head. Whether she was incredibly resilient. Or just plain crazy. I don't know. Either or both. Who can say? But whichever … I'd have to say. What the audience heard was one thing. What she heard was something else. What she heard was…! *(Instead of completing his sentence he begins the introduction to the "Ave Maria." As if summoned by the music, FFJ returns. She sings; beautifully, simply, her tone pure, the line supple and strong —)*
FFJ.

Ave Maria,
Gratia plena,
Dominus tecum:
Benedicta tu.
In mulieribus,
Et Benedictus
Fructus ventris tui, Jesus.
Sancta Maria! Sancta Maria!
Maria!
Ora pro nobis,
Nobis peccatoribus,
Nunc et in hora,

In hora mortis nostrae,
Amen! Amen!
(As she sings she is wrapped in a light that grows increasingly bright till
her radiant expression is all we see. As the song is ending, the light loses
its intensity, bathing her in an amber afterglow till that too is gone and
the stage is left in darkness.)

The Play is Over

PROPERTY LIST

Sheet music
Hat, bag, gloves
Victrola, record
Maraca
Fan

SOUND EFFECTS

Applause
Cheers
Laughter

NEW PLAYS

★ **GUARDIANS by Peter Morris.** In this unflinching look at war, a disgraced American soldier discloses the truth about Abu Ghraib prison, and a clever English journalist reveals how he faked a similar story for the London tabloids. "Compelling, sympathetic and powerful." *–NY Times.* "Sends you into a state of moral turbulence." *–Sunday Times (UK).* "Nothing short of remarkable." *–Village Voice.* [1M, 1W] ISBN: 978-0-8222-2177-7

★ **BLUE DOOR by Tanya Barfield.** Three generations of men (all played by one actor), from slavery through Black Power, challenge Lewis, a tenured professor of mathematics, to embark on a journey combining past and present. "A teasing flare for words." *–Village Voice.* "Unfailingly thought-provoking." *–LA Times.* "The play moves with the speed and logic of a dream." *–Seattle Weekly.* [2M] ISBN: 978-0-8222-2209-5

★ **THE INTELLIGENT DESIGN OF JENNY CHOW by Rolin Jones.** This irreverent "techno-comedy" chronicles one brilliant woman's quest to determine her heritage and face her fears with the help of her astounding creation called Jenny Chow. "Boldly imagined." *–NY Times.* "Fantastical and funny." *–Variety.* "Harvests many laughs and finally a few tears." *–LA Times.* [3M, 3W] ISBN: 978-0-8222-2071-8

★ **SOUVENIR by Stephen Temperley.** Florence Foster Jenkins, a wealthy society eccentric, suffers under the delusion that she is a great coloratura soprano—when in fact the opposite is true. "Hilarious and deeply touching. Incredibly moving and breathtaking." *–NY Daily News.* "A sweet love letter of a play." *–NY Times.* "Wildly funny. Completely charming." *–Star-Ledger.* [1M, 1W] ISBN: 978-0-8222-2157-9

★ **ICE GLEN by Joan Ackermann.** In this touching period comedy, a beautiful poetess dwells in idyllic obscurity on a Berkshire estate with a band of unlikely cohorts. "A beautifully written story of nature and change." *–Talkin' Broadway.* "A lovely play which will leave you with a lot to think about." *–CurtainUp.* "Funny, moving and witty." *–Metroland (Boston).* [4M, 3W] ISBN: 978-0-8222-2175-3

★ **THE LAST DAYS OF JUDAS ISCARIOT by Stephen Adly Guirgis.** Set in a time-bending, darkly comic world between heaven and hell, this play reexamines the plight and fate of the New Testament's most infamous sinner. "An unforced eloquence that finds the poetry in lowdown street talk." *–NY Times.* "A real jaw-dropper." *–Variety.* "An extraordinary play." *–Guardian (UK).* [10M, 5W] ISBN: 978-0-8222-2082-4

DRAMATISTS PLAY SERVICE, INC.
440 Park Avenue South, New York, NY 10016 212-683-8960 Fax 212-213-1539
postmaster@dramatists.com www.dramatists.com

NEW PLAYS

★ **THE GREAT AMERICAN TRAILER PARK MUSICAL music and lyrics by David Nehls, book by Betsy Kelso.** Pippi, a stripper on the run, has just moved into Armadillo Acres, wreaking havoc among the tenants of Florida's most exclusive trailer park. "Adultery, strippers, murderous ex-boyfriends, Costco and the Ice Capades. Undeniable fun." –*NY Post.* "Joyful and unashamedly vulgar." –*The New Yorker.* "Sparkles with treasure." –*New York Sun.* [2M, 5W] ISBN: 978-0-8222-2137-1

★ **MATCH by Stephen Belber.** When a young Seattle couple meet a prominent New York choreographer, they are led on a fraught journey that will change their lives forever. "Uproariously funny, deeply moving, enthralling theatre." –*NY Daily News.* "Prolific laughs and ear-to-ear smiles." –*NY Magazine.* [2M, 1W] ISBN: 978-0-8222-2020-6

★ **MR. MARMALADE by Noah Haidle.** Four-year-old Lucy's imaginary friend, Mr. Marmalade, doesn't have much time for her—not to mention he has a cocaine addiction and a penchant for pornography. "Alternately hilarious and heartbreaking." –*The New Yorker.* "A mature and accomplished play." –*LA Times.* "Scathingly observant comedy." –*Miami Herald.* [4M, 2W] ISBN: 978-0-8222-2142-5

★ **MOONLIGHT AND MAGNOLIAS by Ron Hutchinson.** Three men cloister themselves as they work tirelessly to reshape a screenplay that's just not working—*Gone with the Wind.* "Consumers of vintage Hollywood insider stories will eat up Hutchinson's diverting conjecture." –*Variety.* "A lot of fun." –*NY Post.* "A Hollywood dream-factory farce." –*Chicago Sun-Times.* [3M, 1W] ISBN: 978-0-8222-2084-8

★ **THE LEARNED LADIES OF PARK AVENUE by David Grimm, translated and freely adapted from Molière's *Les Femmes Savantes*.** Dicky wants to marry Betty, but her mother's plan is for Betty to wed a most pompous man. "A brave, brainy and barmy revision." –*Hartford Courant.* "A rare but welcome bird in contemporary theatre." –*New Haven Register.* "Roll over Cole Porter." –*Boston Globe.* [5M, 5W] ISBN: 978-0-8222-2135-7

★ **REGRETS ONLY by Paul Rudnick.** A sparkling comedy of Manhattan manners that explores the latest topics in marriage, friendships and squandered riches. "One of the funniest quip-meisters on the planet." –*NY Times.* "Precious moments of hilarity. Devastatingly accurate political and social satire." –*BackStage.* "Great fun." –*CurtainUp.* [3M, 3W] ISBN: 978-0-8222-2223-1

DRAMATISTS PLAY SERVICE, INC.
440 Park Avenue South, New York, NY 10016 212-683-8960 Fax 212-213-1539
postmaster@dramatists.com www.dramatists.com

NEW PLAYS

★ **AFTER ASHLEY by Gina Gionfriddo.** A teenager is unwillingly thrust into the national spotlight when a family tragedy becomes talk-show fodder. "A work that virtually any audience would find accessible." *–NY Times.* "Deft characterization and caustic humor." *–NY Sun.* "A smart satirical drama." *–Variety.* [4M, 2W] ISBN: 978-0-8222-2099-2

★ **THE RUBY SUNRISE by Rinne Groff.** Twenty-five years after Ruby struggles to realize her dream of inventing the first television, her daughter faces similar battles of faith as she works to get Ruby's story told on network TV. "Measured and intelligent, optimistic yet clear-eyed." *–NY Magazine.* "Maintains an exciting sense of ingenuity." *–Village Voice.* "Sinuous theatrical flair." *–Broadway.com.* [3M, 4W] ISBN: 978-0-8222-2140-1

★ **MY NAME IS RACHEL CORRIE taken from the writings of Rachel Corrie, edited by Alan Rickman and Katharine Viner.** This solo piece tells the story of Rachel Corrie who was killed in Gaza by an Israeli bulldozer set to demolish a Palestinian home. "Heartbreaking urgency. An invigoratingly detailed portrait of a passionate idealist." *–NY Times.* "Deeply authentically human." *–USA Today.* "A stunning dramatization." *–CurtainUp.* [1W] ISBN: 978-0-8222-2222-4

★ **ALMOST, MAINE by John Cariani.** This charming midwinter night's dream of a play turns romantic clichés on their ear as it chronicles the painfully hilarious amorous adventures (and misadventures) of residents of a remote northern town that doesn't quite exist. "A whimsical approach to the joys and perils of romance." *–NY Times.* "Sweet, poignant and witty." *–NY Daily News.* "Aims for the heart by way of the funny bone." *–Star-Ledger.* [2M, 2W] ISBN: 978-0-8222-2156-2

★ **Mitch Albom's TUESDAYS WITH MORRIE by Jeffrey Hatcher and Mitch Albom, based on the book by Mitch Albom.** The true story of Brandeis University professor Morrie Schwartz and his relationship with his student Mitch Albom. "A touching, life-affirming, deeply emotional drama." *–NY Daily News.* "You'll laugh. You'll cry." *–Variety.* "Moving and powerful." *–NY Post.* [2M] ISBN: 978-0-8222-2188-3

★ **DOG SEES GOD: CONFESSIONS OF A TEENAGE BLOCKHEAD by Bert V. Royal.** An abused pianist and a pyromaniac ex-girlfriend contribute to the teen-angst of America's most hapless kid. "A welcome antidote to the notion that the *Peanuts* gang provides merely American cuteness." *–NY Times.* "Hysterically funny." *–NY Post.* "The *Peanuts* kids have finally come out of their shells." *–Time Out.* [4M, 4W] ISBN: 978-0-8222-2152-4

DRAMATISTS PLAY SERVICE, INC.
440 Park Avenue South, New York, NY 10016 212-683-8960 Fax 212-213-1539
postmaster@dramatists.com www.dramatists.com

NEW PLAYS

★ **RABBIT HOLE by David Lindsay-Abaire.** Winner of the 2007 Pulitzer Prize. Becca and Howie Corbett have everything a couple could want until a life-shattering accident turns their world upside down. "An intensely emotional examination of grief, laced with wit." *–Variety.* "A transcendent and deeply affecting new play." *–Entertainment Weekly.* "Painstakingly beautiful." *–BackStage.* [2M, 3W] ISBN: 978-0-8222-2154-8

★ **DOUBT, A Parable by John Patrick Shanley.** Winner of the 2005 Pulitzer Prize and Tony Award. Sister Aloysius, a Bronx school principal, takes matters into her own hands when she suspects the young Father Flynn of improper relations with one of the male students. "All the elements come invigoratingly together like clockwork." *–Variety.* "Passionate, exquisite, important, engrossing." *–NY Newsday.* [1M, 3W] ISBN: 978-0-8222-2219-4

★ **THE PILLOWMAN by Martin McDonagh.** In an unnamed totalitarian state, an author of horrific children's stories discovers that someone has been making his stories come true. "A blindingly bright black comedy." *–NY Times.* "McDonagh's least forgiving, bravest play." *–Variety.* "Thoroughly startling and genuinely intimidating." *–Chicago Tribune.* [4M, 5 bit parts (2M, 1W, 1 boy, 1 girl)] ISBN: 978-0-8222-2100-5

★ **GREY GARDENS book by Doug Wright, music by Scott Frankel, lyrics by Michael Korie.** The hilarious and heartbreaking story of Big Edie and Little Edie Bouvier Beale, the eccentric aunt and cousin of Jacqueline Kennedy Onassis, once bright names on the social register who became East Hampton's most notorious recluses. "An experience no passionate theatergoer should miss." *–NY Times.* "A unique and unmissable musical." *–Rolling Stone.* [4M, 3W, 2 girls] ISBN: 978-0-8222-2181-4

★ **THE LITTLE DOG LAUGHED by Douglas Carter Beane.** Mitchell Green could make it big as the hot new leading man in Hollywood if Diane, his agent, could just keep him in the closet. "Devastatingly funny." *–NY Times.* "An out-and-out delight." *–NY Daily News.* "Full of wit and wisdom." *–NY Post.* [2M, 2W] ISBN: 978-0-8222-2226-2

★ **SHINING CITY by Conor McPherson.** A guilt-ridden man reaches out to a therapist after seeing the ghost of his recently deceased wife. "Haunting, inspired and glorious." *–NY Times.* "Simply breathtaking and astonishing." *–Time Out.* "A thoughtful, artful, absorbing new drama." *–Star-Ledger.* [3M, 1W] ISBN: 978-0-8222-2187-6

DRAMATISTS PLAY SERVICE, INC.
440 Park Avenue South, New York, NY 10016 212-683-8960 Fax 212-213-1539
postmaster@dramatists.com www.dramatists.com